THE CRYING HANDBOOK

For those who always cry,
for those who never do, and
for those who cry somewhere in between

by

Bob Baugher, Ph.D.

&

Darcie Sims, Ph.D.

© 2007

TABLE OF CONTENTS

CHAPTER 1: WHAT IS CRYING?

Introduction

Crying is a mysterious and often misunderstood phenomenon. Crying can be defined as a way to express grief, pain, anger, joy or other emotions by tears, voice or both. We humans secrete a host of fluids that no one wants to see. Tears are pretty much the only secretion that people around us will tolerate; and even then, their acceptance of our crying behavior depends upon many complex factors. You've heard people say, "Crying is normal." Yet, every day people are chastised, criticized, ridiculed and put down for their display of tears—or lack of them. How much do we really know about this human response? Who cries and why? Who doesn't cry and why?

This book was written to help you gain some insight into the mystery of tears. It provides research on what we know and are still learning about crying. We have chosen to look at crying from the other side of the tissue box—the lighter side. We don't think that reading this will cause you to cry, but if you do, go for it. We both have shed our own rivers of tears and invite you to join us on this journey.

Crying Myths

• Myth #1: Crying is a sign of weakness.

This is truly a cultural attitude not a truth. Crying is an individual response to a physiological, emotional, or spiritual state of being and is neither a sign of weakness nor strength. Crying for some requires great strength and courage while for others, not crying requires the same things. For some, crying or not crying comes easily.

• Myth #2: Crying shows you care.

Tears are often used as a measure of how much a person cares. Because people don't cry, does this mean they don't care? Some people cry many tears and care little while others care deeply and remain dry-eyed. Don't let tears or lack of them mislead you.

• Myth #3: Once crying starts, it will never stop.

Many people fear that, once they start crying, they will never stop. As far as we know (and after having consulted the *Guinness Book of World Records*) no one has ever continued crying forever. The fact is at some point, everyone stops crying.

• Myth #4: There is only *one way* to have a "good cry."

What is the definition of a "good cry"? Is a "good cry" one of those tearful displays that involves leaking eyes, a twitching mouth, a runny nose and strange noises coming from the person doing the crying? Or does a "good cry" mean one of those quiet, almost hidden releases of several tears down the cheek--"good" meaning not "creating a scene"?

The Crying Handbook

For some, the physical relief of crying often leads to a less stressful state and in that way, crying is "good" because one feels a bit better when the emotions are released rather than allowed to accumulate within one's body. For others, however, a "good cry" would be considered to be showing as little emotion as possible. It is a message that many have heard most of their lives, couched as "good girls don't cry" or "big boys don't cry". So a "good cry" would be a hidden release or no release at all. This myth is derived from Freudian theory, which supports an overflow view of crying. Crying is seen as a kind of safety valve, whereby an emotional buildup reaches a threshold and crying releases it [1]. The people who support this approach use phrases such as:

Go ahead, get the tears out.
Crying is good for you.
Crying is a release.

Conversely we also hear phrases that caution against *not* crying
If you don't cry, it'll just feel worse.
Stuffing your tears is unhealthy.
People who don't cry end up with all sorts of physical problems.

Because many people do not cry on the "outside" or do not find relief in crying, it is important not to judge their definition of a "good cry."

• Myth #5: One *has* to cry in order to heal.

Any time we see the phrase "has to" or "must," we lean back with caution. Who wrote that rule? And what does it mean to "heal"? Does it mean: Get over it? Get through it? Recover from it? Forget it? Not be bothered by it any more? Emotions are personal and how we express and experience them is a reflection of our uniqueness. There must be a million "prescriptions" for how to "heal," and crying is only one of them.

A Description of Crying

L.B. Lofgren [2] provided an interesting description of crying:

At the beginning of the process the person may look away, blink and show a sniffling jerk. If the process continues, the person's chin may tremble and the lips may purse. The person may be unable to talk or the voice may quiver. With further progression, respiration begins a series of short, irregular, deep and gasping expirations. The face shows crinkling of the features, puckering of the brow and downward force of the mouth. The shoulders may slump forward and redness and puffiness may fill the face.

Our Description

Or you might enjoy this description we came up with based upon our years of experience watching people cry:

At the beginning the person may have a faraway look, like the kind you see when you forgot the answer to a simple question, such as "What is your name?" This is followed by the nose moving upward toward the eyes giving a snout-like appearance. This causes squinting, blinking, clouding vision and an overall attempt toward blindness to the incoming bad news. The chin and lips may vibrate at 5-6 cycles per second as the intended words "What's happening" come out as "Whaa-whaa-whaa." As the brain feels its blood drain, its need for oxygen kicks in, causing gasping for breath. If crying continues to its crescendo, the person's wailing brings people walking by to stare and wonder, "What's going on?"

The Crying Scale

A way to understand the progression of crying is to look at The Crying Scale below. See how far you've gotten in the recent past:

1. Chest and/or throat tighten, but no evidence of tears ("crying on the inside")
2. Eyes moisten
3. Tears well up, but do not fall
4. Tears well up, but do fall
5. Tears well up, many fall
6. Tears, some sobbing
7. Tears, much sobbing
8. Tears, sobbing, wailing
9. Tears, sobbing, screaming (possibly accompanied by falling to one's knees)
10. All of the above and more

If this is too much to remember, here is a summary of the scale:

Tighten

Tears

Titanic

Measuring Crying: Frequency or Proneness?

In the literature on crying, the experts make a critical distinction between two ways that crying has been measured. One is *Crying Frequency*, meaning simply "How often have you cried during, say, the past month?" The other is *Crying Proneness*, which refers to situations that prompt crying, such as thinking of a recent breakup, watching a movie, visiting a place. So, you might be the type of person who is prone to cry, but if you avoid those tear-triggering situations your Crying Frequency would be low. On the other hand, you might not be the type of person who has a number trigger points, but if you are faced with those one or two special triggers you might be crying several times a week. Make sense?

Let's look at an example:

Crynelda is crying-prone. In her crying diary she has listed the following triggers: Five songs, looking at pictures of her former boyfriend, Thanksgiving (the day her boyfriend broke up with her), telling someone the story of the day her boyfriend left her and donuts.

Do you see that, with the exception of Thanksgiving, it is entirely possible for Crynelda to go through an entire year without crying? She could choose not to play the five songs. Crynelda could burn her ex-boyfriend's pictures. She could refuse to talk about him. However, avoiding Thanksgiving and her beloved donuts just isn't practical. She will always remember the chocolate-glazed moment of love when she met him at the donut shop. And she will never forget the mess at the family Thanksgiving when he said "Crynelda...I realize I have something to be thankful for... I'm leaving you." Those "triggers" will probably always bring tears. She is highly crying-prone, but her frequency could be near zero if she laid off the donuts and skipped Turkey Day.

Laughter and Tears—Tough to Study

Do people who cry from joy feel even better afterwards or just the same? In a conversation with Bill Frey, author of *Crying: The Mystery of Tears*, he stated that he attempted to set up a study in which people would "laugh so hard they cried" but was unable to find anything that could reliably produce such a response. Because of this, to this day there is little research on the role of laughter and tears. He further stated that he has often been misquoted in saying that tears of sadness were chemically different from tears of joy. As of this date we just don't know.

A Brief History of Crying

In American pre-Victorian times (1700s-1800s) the expectation was that of moderation. That is, if you cried too much, it signified an excessive focus on the here and now and too little faith in the world beyond. In the Victorian age they saw death as failure of medicine and loss of ties with family, which prompted many tears. Grief became expressive and often excessive. In the early 1900s, the emergence of World War I brought renewed restraint. Crying was considered a backward-looking emotion [3]. Maintaining a "stiff upper lip" became the expectation in American society.

Today, crying has many mixed messages. Men are encouraged to cry but when they do, no one knows how to respond. Women who don't cry may be considered to be "cold and uncaring." Crying in public is tolerable as long as we look like we are trying not to; but public crying is still less acceptable than crying in private. Often we don't know what to do when someone starts to cry...Pat? Hug? Offer a tissue? Pretend not to notice? Or just let them cry?

Words that Describe Crying

Sociologists tell us that one way to understand how a society interprets a phenomenon is to examine the words used to describe it. Synonyms for cry are:

weep	keen	moan	shed tears
wail	bawl	sob	
whimper	snivel	howl	

Related terms are:

falling apart	breaking down
losing it	being a wimp.

However, the one that seems to carry the most negative connotation is blubber. Look back at the list. Would American society consider any of these positive? Would you like to be considered a crybaby, a person who whimpers, someone who is falling apart, or worse: a blubberer?

It is a sad commentary about our culture when something as natural as crying has so few positive descriptors. The closest term we have to depicting crying in a positive way is "a good cry." One other thing, when people cry, they often apologize for their tears. Think about it. We have just been moved by something that has revealed our innermost feelings and we say, "I'm sorry"?

Here's an alternate proposal: Let's create "National Crying Day" where we remind people that it's okay to cry and you do not have to apologize for your tears. Perhaps one of the greatest lessons of National Crying Day would be an increase of acceptability and tolerance for crying and tears. A powerful example of this need for toleance is the research finding that (so-called) "excessive" crying in children is one of the major triggers of child abuse by parents and other caregivers [4, 5]. Perhaps the more people learn about crying, the more they will learn to tolerate it. We may even see the creation of words that describe crying in a positive way—but don't hold your breath.

CHAPTER 2: RESEARCH ON CRYING

(Special thanks to editors Dr. Ad J.J.M. Vingerhoets and Dr. Randolph R. Cornelius and their contributors to the book *Adult Crying: A Biopsychosocial Approach* for the research their book provided.)

The Biochemical Approach to Crying

Did you know that the components of tears are proteins, enzymes, lipids, metabolites and electrolytes? [6] Go ahead, impress your friends. Bring it up at dinner by saying something like, "Yes, well the other day when I was crying I thought, hmm, there goes a slew of proteins, enzymes, lipids, metabolites and electrolytes right out of my eyeballs. And please pass the black-eyed peas.".

In his book *Crying: The Natural & Cultural History of Tears* [7] Tom Lutz noted that physiologists categorize tears in three ways: Basal—the tears that continuously lubricate, Reflex—those that react to an irritant such as an onion and Psychic—those related to emotions.

All three of these types of tears are secreted by the lacrimal glands, which are located near the outside corners of your eyes. On the inside corners, next to your nose are holes where tears can drain into the nasal cavity—which is often the reason that, after crying, a person might say, "Can you hand me about twenty tissues, please?"

In 1981 William Frey and his associates [8] found that the protein concentration of psychic tears was 24% greater than reflex tears. He later hypothesized that crying served as a means of eliminating hormones such as prolactin, ACTH and Leucine-enkephalin which are known to be released from the pituitary gland and enter the blood in response to stress [9]. So, the next time you see someone crying go up and say, "Hey, good for you. You've just successfully reduced prolactin, ACTH and Leucine-enkephalin. Great job at lowering your stress!"

Two researchers, Lensvelt & Vingerhoets, [10] found a genetic basis for Crying Proneness in studying identical and nonidentical female twins. So, ladies, (and perhaps men, too) your proneness to cry in response to a number of triggers has a degree of inheritability. If you are the type of person who cries during the first few seconds of *Bambi* or *The Lion King*, blame it partly on your genes or your family tree. On the other hand, if your eyes hardly glisten during the entire movie, don't fight it, your genes are showing.

Emotional Expression—High, Medium, or Low?

Some people express few emotions. Quick, think of a person in your life who is like that. Say his or her name in your mind. Why would you think this person doesn't express emotions? Vinger-hoets and his associates [11] pointed out three reasons that seem to be involved. See if any make sense to you:

One reason is because *this person is not aware of his or her internal emotional reaction.* Consider a person's awareness of their emotions on a scale from total unawareness to total awareness. See the scale below:

| Totally Unaware | Some Awareness | Totally Aware |

When people are asked, "So, how do you *feel* about that?" some people can reel off a number of emotions: "Well, Tom, at first I was a little apprehensive but hopeful. Later I was excited, motivated, happy, but fearful, too." Pretty good, huh? Six emotions in a matter of seconds. For other people the answer is not so verbose: "Um, I don't know. A little weird, I guess. It's just a weird feeling. That's all."

In our interactions with others, we need to recognize that we are all wired differently and accept those differences. Of course you knew that already. But when it comes to expressing or identifying emotional content, we sometimes forget and want everyone we know to "express themselves." Some folks out there score way to the left (totally unaware) on the emotional awareness scale and that's the best they can do.

Another reason for lack of emotional expression is because the person *doesn't want others to know.* Have you ever stopped yourself from crying because you wanted to hide your feelings? Was that a rule in your family? Who serves as the "rock" in your family now? You know, the person who is expected to be strong, especially when a crisis hits? Imagine this person crying in the middle of a family crisis. You get the idea. Sometimes a family member steps forward to be the strong one. In other families the "rock" is *appointed*—often without a vote. In either case most family members do not want to see their "rock" crying, weeping and wailing whenever strength is needed at the time. Family rules can often dictate how comfortable we are in expressing our emotions.

A third reason for lack of emotional expression is because *the person filters incoming information.* Have your ever turned off the television because the information coming through was too painful, overwhelming, or distasteful? Our brains can handle only so much discomfort. When we reach overload, we engage in any number of behaviors to decrease or block the painful input.

Examples are:

- Escape (turning off the television)
- Avoidance (not turning it on in the first place)
- Denying (it's not really happening)
- Rationalization (it's not really *that* bad)
- Emotional insulation (hiding from your feelings rather than acknowledging them)

Some people do this "filtering" process often because they cannot take in any (more) negative input whereas other people "filter" less often because they are able to handle the discomfort and pain. It is important to understand that it is often easy to criticize a person who constantly blocks incoming negative input as "heartless." Perhaps that person is already on overload from a past full of negative experiences. Also, don't forget the earlier discussion we had regarding the physiological approach to crying. Some people are wired to be overly sensitive to all incoming negative, or in some cases, even positive input—so even a small amount is perceived as too much.

Another reason for filtering is exposure to dramatic or traumatic stressors all of which have the capacity to cause emotional numbness. Sometimes you are just too frozen to cry.

In summary, people may not appear to be emotional because they are unaware, don't want other people to know, or are "filtering" the input. One more thing: Just because a person is unemotional doesn't necessarily make him or her a noncrier. Conversely, a highly emotional person is not necessarily a big crier. Tears may or may not be an accurate reflection of a person's emotional state.

Crying Time

If you cry, when does it happen? In the morning, at work, at night? Findings from several sources have concluded that crying increased from four a.m. to a peak between eight and eleven p.m. [12, 13, 14, 15]. Why between eight and eleven p.m.? Is this true for you? Is it because:

- you are alone? (at last!)?
- you are tired and your "filters" are thin (your defenses are lowered)?
- something on television or the internet triggered you?
- you are interacting with a person who may be the cause of your tears?
- you are with someone with whom you feel safe?

In fact research has shown that people are more likely to cry when they are alone and that 75% of crying takes place at home [14, 15]. In our culture crying tends to be a private matter.

Crying without Warning

Have you ever been surprised by your tears? Vingerhoets [13] found in 11% of cases people were surprised at their own tears. Let's say you had a run-in with a relative (we won't mention any names, you know the one we're talking about). No tears were shed at the time; but a couple hours later you are talking with a friend about the run-in and—bam—suddenly you're leaking. Now, how did that happen?

Research [16] on lacrimal flow, in which they measured the actual tear flow of people while they were experiencing various emotions (such as joy and sadness), showed that many of us—especially women—experience changes in mood without our conscious awareness. In other words you might have been more upset with your relative at the time than you realized. What's the point in this? Pay attention to your tears. If your tears are flowing, this may be a sign that you are more affected by the experience than you first thought.

- Maria suddenly found herself crying as she watched a beautiful sunset and realized she had no one with which to share it.

- Anthony found himself staring out the kitchen window, watching his two children play. Suddenly he realized tears were streaming down his cheeks. How could he be so lucky?

Do We Cry for Unconscious Reasons? Here Are Two Examples:

- In 2005 Bob visited South Africa for the first time and as the plane was landing in Johannesburg, he thought he might cry for finally having reached a lifelong goal to visit Africa. But he didn't. Five days later, while visiting a township, Bob was suddenly and surprisingly moved to tears when folks at a senior center rose up from their chairs and began singing as a way to thank him and the other visitors for coming.

- Sara walked into work and a special song was playing on the radio. She hurried to the restroom to dry her tears. Where did *they* come from?

When did your tears last surprise you?

Good Tears—Bad Tears

Tom Lutz [7] made an interesting distinction between tears. So-called "good" tears are those cried for pleasure (tears from laughter), sincerity (honest, genuine, authentic tears) and heroism (tears cried in response to a great deed). One type of "bad" tears are those cried from self-indulgence, such as when we feel the person is "overreacting" to pain—think of a child who screams out after being merely tapped by his older brother or the losing players on an underdog sports team. Few people have sympathy for such behavior.

Another type of "bad" tears are those of insincerity. Have you ever felt that someone was crying as a way to manipulate you? They want something and they turn on the faucet. Tears, sobs, drool and sniffles of anguish beseech us, drawing us into their web of guilt, all orchestrated to get the prize they so desire. The moment the prize is either received or if we refuse to respond appropriately, off goes the faucet. Lutz pointed out the origin of the term "crocodile tears" by explaining that tears are squeezed out of the creature only when the jaws are fully extended to engulf the victim. Sound familiar? Few of us want to be manipulated and when tears are the vehicle, most people feel betrayed.

How Does Your Brain Deal With Crying?—The Cognitive Approach

There is an interesting term for the way our mind handles incoming information. It is called *schema*. This cognitive approach refers to a cluster of related   ideas around a topic that is carried in the brain. If we see something that far exceeds the boundaries of our schema (our view of the world), we don't know how to make sense of it. We struggle to find a way to assimilate it, reject it, or begin to create a new view.

Labott and Martin [17]) point out that, when we cry (for example at hearing or experiencing the death of a loved one) it signals that we have begun to give up our original schema—that our loved one is alive and well. Here is a way to think about crying from a cognitive perspective:

We are more likely to cry when a highly arousing event occurs in our lives that we cannot incorporate into any of our existing schemas (worldviews).

We cry because we are *helpless* to maintain our original *schema*. This feeling of helplessness is supported by the fact that we tend to cry at some point <u>after</u> the peak of an emotion [7]. Once the emotion begins to subside and our helplessness grows, our tears may come.

Denial can be understood as a form of hanging on to our original view. Think of a person you love. How many memories of this person do you have stored in your brain? A thousand? A hundred thousand? Millions? Now, imagine that you have just heard this person has died. You have no schema for this. You deny. But, as the reality sets in—for example, if you see this person's body—you may begin to deny less and begin to realize that the death is real. You feel the loss as you start to helplessly relinquish some of your original schema. This may be the time when you first begin to cry. Because the crying process can shift our attention from our thoughts and our emotions to our bodies, crying can begin to alleviate some of our emotional pain [7]. For some people it occurs immediately. For others there is continued shock or numbness, which contributes to a delay in feeling the loss—and a delay of tears.

Crying as a Social Phenomenon

Think of the last time when you cried with other people around you. Did you want them to know what you were feeling? As the tears were streaming down your face, what did you want the people to do? Ignore you? Hug you? Talk with you? Encourage you to dry your eyes? Tell you everything would be okay? Just be with you?

In his book *The Language of Tears* Jeffrey Kottler [18] focused on the communicative nature of crying as a way of soliciting help. A baby cries when wet, hungry or bored and needs your help. Have you ever cried and wanted someone to come help you? Or have your tears sent a "Leave me alone" message? Sometimes crying is a way to say "I give up." When the people who know you see you cry, do they know exactly what to do? Crying often delivers mixed messages and everyone may feel confused and helpless.

Have you ever cried because someone else was crying? This is called *emotional contagion*. [19, 20]. One reason we do it is because we feel empathy and we cry because of the other person's pain. Another reason is because the tears we see in the other person are a reflection of our own pain. These are the tears of sincerity we discussed earlier. Think back to the last time you cried with others. For many people, this is a powerful moment. In crying together we are agreeing on what is most important [7].

Crying as a Spiritual Connection

In addition to the social and cognitive approaches, tears sometimes flow from a person's experiences with their spiritual connection. Hearing or singing a favorite spiritual song, reading from a holy book, or simply engaging in prayer can move a person to tears. Or sometimes it is just being in the presence of something beyond one's self that inspires tears of awe.

Where Do People Cry?

For some people, one of the major factors that influences where they allow themselves to cry is the fear of loss of control. As noted earlier the majority of crying episodes occur at home. Aside from the obvious situation in which place is irrelevant, such as learning of the death of a loved one, other places people are more likely to cry include: weddings, sports events, funeral homes, churches, cemeteries and movies.

Interestingly, research has shown that even the most powerful movie scenes have been able to elicit tears in only one-third of women [21]. So, if you find yourself crying the next time you're in a theatre and glance around to see you're in the minority, don't worry, only some of the audience is on the same wave (tear) length.

Kottler reminds us that we actually pay good money to sit in a darkened movie theatre with strangers just so that we can cry, wipe tears and blow our nose. Would you still do this if the lights were on and a giant mirror were in front so everyone could see each other? We may cry at the movies because it is a private space in a public place.

Crying on the Big Screen—What Is the Message?

The next time you watch a movie, notice an incident of crying and ask, "What message is the director trying to convey?" It is   a rare movie in which we are exposed to more than a few seconds of sobbing or more than 30 seconds of tears. Referring to the Crying Scale on page 5, if we see any tears on the screen we typically see them welling up, but not falling (step 3); but in a few cases tears do fall (step 4). We almost never experience step 5 (many tears fall). Instead we see our hero or heroine in what is clearly the depths of grief, but only at step 3 or 4. Think about it: attempting to conceal one's tears *is* considered an act of heroism. If our hero were to fall on the ground sobbing, would this act lose our respect?

One exception to the trend of stopping at step 3 or 4 is a cemetery scene from the movie "Steel Magnolias" in which Sally Field, who plays the mother of a young woman about to be buried, begins to cry. The scene is a powerful one in which she sobs, wails and expresses rage (step 8). This may be one of the longest depictions of raw grief. What is the length of this epic segment in a film of nearly two hours? Seventy-one seconds! We can only assume that this time period may be the maximum that viewers are able to tolerate. Of course we cannot have an entire movie of crying. Or can we? Would you sit through two hours of nothing but tears, snot, wailing and screaming? We don't think so.

Differences in Crying

Think of a container that stores all our emotions. Our level of emotional arousal grows as we are bombarded with the stressors and joys of daily life. When our life gets too crazy, the container splashes around spilling excess liquid expressed as tears [7]. Some of us are born with small containers. It doesn't take much to overflow. Others have larger containers or learn methods for balancing and adjusting to the bumps and insults of the external world. Some have learned to keep a tight lid on their container. Yet, some containers are already brimming with liquid waiting for the least little nudge to spill over in tears. What does your container look like at this point in your life? How full is it?

Every culture has ***expectations of behavior*** for its different populations. And culture is more than ethnicity. There is the culture of age, the culture of gender, the culture of location (church, grocery store, home, workplace, cemetery), the culture of relationship and connection (parent, child, best friend, enemy).

Every culture has specific rules, boundaries and expectations for the shedding of tears. Each culture dictates which gender is expected to cry and defines the ages at which crying is most acceptable. In your own culture, what is the eldest age it is still acceptable to cry? Five? Ten? Seventy-five? In our culture, it is acceptable for children and for the elderly to cry, but less acceptable for the young and middle-aged adult to do so. Did you ever notice that people in their sixties and older have fewer tears when they cry? The next time this happens you can say to this person, "Hey, it looks like your lacrimal glands are getting a little dry."

Where one cries is also culturally bound. In some cultures, crying in public is never acceptable while in others, those who do not publicly express their tears are considered to be "cold," "unresponsive" or even worse, "don't care." In the United States, crying following the death of a loved one is expected to move from public display to private anguish after three or four days, a week at most. Is it because we are so uncomfortable with someone crying? Do we feel helpless and powerless to help them or to comfort them? Do we wish they would feel better *now* or just stop the crying because we are close to tears ourselves?

Culture and Crying

In his research with the Toraja tribe in Indonesia, Wellenkamp [22] found that it is against tribal tradition for adults to cry (audibly) except in two instances: after a death and during a funeral or a secondary burial or if a female is unable to conceive. This ban on crying is equivalent in severity to the sanction against adultery and cursing someone. Crying does occur in other situations (e.g. during arguments). If this happens, the person must make a sacrificial offering as a gesture of compensation.

The vast majority of studies have been conducted in Western cultures, more specifically the U.S. and Northern Europe. In the International Study on Adult Crying [23] participants from 29 other countries were asked how often they had cried in the previous four weeks and what triggered it. Although cultural differences in both crying frequency and crying proneness seemed to emerge, the authors of the study concluded that the complexity of cultural definitions of crying frequency and crying situations made the results difficult to interpret. An example of this difficulty is shown in cultures that place high sanctions against male tears. Because males in these cultures are less likely to admit to crying, it is difficult to assess their crying frequency and proneness. Therefore, we can only speculate which countries expel the most tears.

Kottler [18] stated that, in North America, socioeconomic status (social class, occupation and education) is a better predictor of crying than cultural and religious background. That is, a person is more likely to cry, regardless of culture if he or she has the following characteristics:

- a higher education
- a flexible set of gender roles
- a people-oriented job

Gender Differences in Crying

Research on the biology of tears [24, 25] found that levels of serum prolactin (which stimulates tear production) are similar in girls and boys up to age 16 after which female levels exceed males. These levels also increase during pregnancy. In another study [26] twelve-year-old females averaged 1.9 crying episodes per week while males averaged 1.8 per week. The definition of crying was "at least watery eyes." After age twelve boys began to show greater declines.

Frey [27] conducted a study in 1983 in which he asked 286 females and 45 males ages 18-75 to keep crying diaries. Females averaged 5.3 crying episodes a month while males averaged 1.4. Kottler [18] stated that about 80% of men reported that they never or hardly ever cried compared to 80% of women who reported crying on a regular basis.

In questioning why people cry, Williams and Morris [28] surveyed English and Israeli university students. They found that females cried more often in conflict and anger situations while male tears flowed more easily than females when experiencing positive events. Some feminists contend that women are forced to use crying because of their lack of access to other forms of power [7].

In summary, several studies support the finding that women cry more frequently and more intensely than men. Regarding Crying Proneness, the likelihood that someone will cry in the presence of an external stimulus (watching a sad movie, seeing someone cry, hearing bad news) or an emotion (anger, sadness, joy), women still show higher scores than men. Further research is needed to determine whether women also cry for longer durations. Men may not only attempt to swallow their tears, they may have fewer tear-provoking experiences, or they may avoid situations that they know are likely to make them cry.

Kottler [18] pointed out that our society labels noncrying men as insensitive; but most of these judgments are made using women's standards for emotional display. Today's man gets mixed messages: be strong, yet sensitive. More specifically, men should strive to be successfully competitive at work, but tender at home. Cindy Chupack [29] said it well, women "like a man who's not afraid to cry...but doesn't." On the other hand, when *men* see someone cry, they get "logical," they want to "fix" it.

In his discussion of gender differences Lutz pointed to the popular myth that men have been crippled by growing up to learn that crying is a sign of weakness; and because they don't cry these poor guys are destined to become aggressive, are unable to be intimate and nurturing and cannot "get in touch with their feelings." As a result, he continues, women end up doing the emotional work for men by taking on more than their share of emotional expression. Lutz concluded that, in fact, there is no historical basis for arguing that men should cry more or women should cry less as a way to bring a power balance between the sexes.

We know that men do cry; however, like women, men are bound by cultural rules. Consider the example from Cindy Chupak [29] in her article from 1994 *Glamour* magazine: think how you would respond to a man who sheds tears as the woman in his life glides down the staircase proudly displaying her new dress. Then think how you would feel about the same man crying over an unbalanced checkbook. Women also have their own cultural restrictions on crying. For example, females who are politicians, government officials, supervisors, CEOs and in other positions of power experience heavy sanctions against tear shedding. Kottler noted that no one seems to be very happy with society's expectations of crying. Both men *and* women experience a prohibition against being too emotional.

Crying and Laughing—Are They Similar?

For most people, both crying and laughing can provide a release. The physical movement of some parts of the body, particularly the lungs and diaphragm, are similar during both a cry and a laugh. Here's a story example:

Years ago Bob audiotaped a counseling session with a client. During their discussion the client did a great deal of intense crying (up to Step 7: tears, much sobbing). She had planned to take the tape home, but it broke during the session. Later that week Bob took it home and asked his teenage son, Shawn, to repair it with the caution not to listen to the tape due to counselor/client confidentiality. A couple of days later Bob heard sobbing from Shawn's room. Upon opening the door, when Bob saw Shawn standing next to the tape recorder he sternly stated, "I told you not to listen to my client's tape."

Shawn replied, "I haven't fixed the tape yet. See? I copied this other tape from a video. It is the sound of the next-door neighbor lady laughing hysterically at our last year's party. I slowed it down to one-half speed and it sounds like someone crying."

He was right: What Bob thought was a tape of a person sobbing was actually a person laughing at one-half speed! It was then that he became even more convinced of the similarity between laughing and crying.

We have all seen people cry, then laugh and laugh, then cry. It may not be that laughter is a substitute for a good cry, but it is clear that they indeed have much in common.

As we saw in the example above, both crying and laughing bring about similar body responses. In addition, Cornelius [1] suggested that a feeling of helplessness is common to both.

Have you ever laughed so hard that you began to cry? Or have you ever cried so hard that you began to laugh? So maybe tears and laughter are really closer than we know. Perhaps laughter and tears come from the same place—somewhere deep inside of us.

CHAPTER 3: CRYING: MORE OR LESS

Suppressing the Cry

In addition to avoiding crying triggers, another reason for tearlessness is suppression of the crying response. One effective way of doing this is swallowing. Another way is aerobic exercise or changing the focus of your thoughts. Here are examples of each:

Swallowing: Marcella is a sergeant in the Army. When she first entered she realized how important it was to suppress her crying. She stated, "During times when things get rough and I begin to feel a cry coming on, I swallow and I mean *hard*. If I have liquid handy I'll pick it up and start guzzling it down. It doesn't feel too good, but it works when I need it."

Aerobics: When Roberto was 44 his father died of a sudden heart attack. Roberto reflects on the day after: "It was horrible for us to lose Dad like this—and it was so sudden. But the next day I went for my Wednesday morning jog. As I took off I began thinking of him and how much I was missing him and I started crying. It was weird because, as I was running and breathing hard, I found that I couldn't cry at the same time. As soon as I stopped about a half hour later—boom—the crying came right back." Smiling, Roberto added, "I guess if you don't want to weep in front of someone, start running."

Changing Your Focus: For some people thinking of something positive, such as a happy memory or a funny story may be a way of suppressing tears.

Aerobic Swallowing: Try this exercise: swallow as hard and as fast as you can 632 times. You might want to practice in front of a mirror or in the closet before doing this in public. You may end up with the hiccups, but heck, that might be better than crying.

Crying Little or Not at All

In addition to our physiology, another reason for individual differences is due to our upbringing. Here are some common phrases heard in childhood that may contribute to our adult crying level. See if any apply to you:

- Don't be a crybaby
- Stop crying—get over it.
- If you're going to cry about it, go to your room.
- What's the matter? You can't handle it?
- Be a man.
- Shut up. I can't stand your crying.
- You sissy
- Come on, buck up, be strong.
- If you don't stop crying, I'll give you something to cry about.

The following story shows the power of parental statements. *Twenty-seven year old Tino told the story of the time he was six years old and became lost in the mall. Twenty minutes later (it seemed like hours to him), when his father found him in tears, he was scolded and sternly told, "This isn't anything to cry about. I don't want you crying anymore. Grow up."*

Believe it or not, from that day forward, for the next twenty-one years, Tino prided himself on his ability to hold back his tears beginning at the moment in the mall. Two years later, at age

*twenty-nine, Tino found himself in a long-term relationship.
What was his partner's major complaint? His unwillingness (or
perhaps inability) to express his feelings and cry. He reported
that, after a few counseling sessions, he became able to shed
some tears for the first time since that day in the mall. It is still
difficult for him to cry. He now states, "I can do it a little and
that's a start."*

Another reason is based on a fear that goes something like this:
"If I start crying, I'll never be able to stop." This is related to
Myth #3: *Once crying starts, it will never stop.* People
with this belief imagine that, once the dam bursts (a
phrase they often use), the flooding will be so great
that they will lose control. This belief may be related
to the finding, discussed earlier, that crying more
often takes place at home and/or alone. These folks
have a high need for control and they see crying as "breaking
down" and perhaps looking vulnerable. Does this describe anyone
you know?

Types of Crying

There must be a million ways to cry. In fact, crying is so
individualistic that it just might be impossible to categorize crying
types. However, here are a few of our ideas.

Weepers and Wailers. The Weepers and Wailers cry easily.
They cry at "the drop of a hat." In fact, they cry so easily that
they have been known to cry in their sleep! These people cry
when they are happy. They cry when they are sad. They sometimes cry when they are angry or frustrated. Sometimes they cry
when they are scared and even when they are bored. Tear release
is quite easy for the Weepers and Wailers.

They've been called crybabies, blubberers, wimps, overly sensitive and in some cases manipulators. A nicer name is "those who carry their hearts on their sleeve."

They often accompany the stream of tears with some type of noise. Sometimes it is simply sniffling and sometimes it can become an outright *wail*. Some cultures require that the deceased be "wailed across" and Weepers and Wailers are in high demand. Sometimes the WW's fall into the arms of others around them or even fall on top of or *into* the casket at a funeral. Whatever the personal style of the Weeper and Wailer, they are open and demonstrative in their crying and often find relief in the emptying of the tears held inside.

The Silent Slider. The Silent Slider is more reserved and quiet in crying. These people do most of their crying quietly with little fanfare or noise. Tears most often simply begin to slide down the cheek. Sometimes these tears are checked with a finger or back of the hand, but often they are allowed to course their way to the jaw and left to drip off the chin or jaw line. Sometimes the Silent Slider does nothing to stop the stream of tears and just allows them to flow.

They may or may not use a tissue to mop up the dampness. Tiny tear streaks can often later be seen on the cheeks. The Silent Slider can become a Weeper and a Wailer at any moment, but is usually trying hard not to cry or to become a public spectacle.

The Hiccupper. This type of crier often experiences hiccups during a tearing moment. Hiccups usually occur when one is trying to stop the tears and their accompanying sounds (remember *Aerobic Swallowing*?) Holding one's breath will often stop the flow of tears and sounds, but may cause a spasm of the diaphragm, which can result in hiccups. Sometimes the hiccups become quite pronounced, much to the embarrassment of the crier and can cause snickers and laughter in those surrounding the crier. Occasionally the crier will join in the laughter and then realize one can laugh and cry at the same time (and hiccup too).

The "I Don't Cry" Crier - The Non-Crier. Some people just don't cry (or appear to). These non-leakers are often mistakenly believed to be "cold, heartless and uncaring." Nothing could be further from the truth! The vast majority of Non-criers do care and are neither heartless nor "cold." They just don't show their emotions in the same, more familiar ways as most of us.

If they cry at all, Non-criers may cry on the *inside* rather than have a visible flow of tears. For some reason, their tears do not flow down the outside of the cheek, but rather seem to stream inside, where no one else can see them. It is a much more private and contained way of "crying." These people are sometimes the focus of others who believe the myths about crying. People will do all kinds of things in an attempt to get the non-crier to cry. Everyone does not have to cry or cry in the same way.

The Once-in-a-Great-While Crier. The Once-in-a-Great-While Crier cries so infrequently that people begin to wonder "Why does he cry so little?" The best answer is "He's doing the best he can." If you are an infrequent crier, it is important for you to appreciate the combination of reasons (biology and environment) that has contributed to your present crying level. Another reason you are an infrequent crier or even a Non-crier is that you are a swallower in the face of a potentially triggering event. If you want to cry or cry more, don't swallow.

After Crying—Better or Worse?

After you cry, do you feel better, worse, or the same? What do you think most people feel? Don't peek. Take a guess.

If you guessed "feel better" you're correct. In his crying diary study Frey [27] found that 85% of women and 73% of men reported feeling better afterwards. As interesting and predictable as these findings are, consider the fact that since the findings were not 100% it leaves 15% of women and 27% of men who felt no better or even worse. For these folks the idea of experiencing a "good cry" may be foreign to them (remember The Myths?) So, the next time you start to urge someone to cry, keep in mind that this person may be in the minority of those who don't feel better afterwards. In fact, they might say something like, "Oh, thanks for encouraging me to cry—I thought you said I'd feel better."

There is no research on why some folks don't feel better following a crying episode. One reason may be that some people stop their crying in the middle, perhaps out of embarrassment or some other reason. Suppressing or "swallowing down" our crying response tends to produce feelings of discomfort. Other reasons for not feeling better might be experiencing "post-cry headache," disappointment in having "lost control," feeling physically exhausted from extended crying or having been seen by others as being "weak."

Have you ever tried to stop crying and discovered a lump in your throat that felt like the size of a basketball? Did you try to "swallow it down," hold your breath, clench your fists, close your eyes or just attempt to ignore it? Your body is trying to tell you something. Are you listening?

Triggers for Crying

Crying is triggered by many things. These things can be categorized by what you see, hear, smell, taste, or feel. Here are some examples. Can you think of others?

1. Visual

   a. Pictures
   b. Places
   c. Similar faces or situations
   d. Funeral home and cemetery
   e. Activities such as children at play
   f. Anniversaries such as a birthday or the yearly date a loved one died
   g. Holiday sights
   h. Dreams

2. Auditory
   a. Music
   b. Words, phrases
   c. Sounds (yelling, other people crying)

3. Smells
   a. Foods
   b. Perfumes
   c Body odors
   d. Fragrances related to a memory
   e. Smells of nature (flowers, freshly mowed grass, outhouse)

4. Taste
   a. Eating or preparing food
   b. Eating at a restaurant where you have memories
   c. Drinking something

5. Touch
   a. Giving or receiving a hug
   b. Missing being touched
   c. Textures (the feel of material, pet fur, wood)

Other Triggering Events for Crying

Death of loved ones, friends, acquaintances
Experiencing or viewing suffering
Broken love relationships
Reunion following separation from a loved one
Weddings, births
Rituals
Conflicts
Being rejected
Feelings of personal inadequacy
Media, movies, books
Achievements
Receiving a compliment
Receiving a gift (or the wrong gift)
Waking up from a bad dream

Emotions Related to Crying

Arthur Koestler [30] listed five situations in which we are more likely to cry: grief, empathy, self-pity, rapture and relief. Think about it. It is during these times when we are not able to *do* much of anything about our state of affairs. What we are left with is the realization that we can do nothing much beyond experiencing the emotions of the moment. Such feelings that accompany or precede our tears are complex. They often involve a mixture of emotional content such as when we are sad, happy, anxious, frustrated, fearful, or angry.

However, the most common themes that accompany crying are *helplessness* and *powerlessness* [1]. Note that loss is an important event in the majority of emotions related to crying.

Suggestion: Try to make yourself cry without thinking of something sad. Did it feel uncomfortable? Were you even able to do it? While we sometimes cry from rapture and joy, many tears are born in sadness.

Your Personal Rules for Crying

Most people don't think that they have rules for crying, but answer the following questions to determine if you do have crying rules. When and if you cry:

1. Are there certain situations in which you would not cry? Work? School? Church? At a mall? In a park? Walking down the street?
2. Are there certain people you would not want to see you cry?
3. Would you wish to be with another person when you cry or would you rather cry alone?
4. If someone is with you when you cry, would it be okay if this person looked at you or would you rather they looked away?
5. Have your ever felt that your crying has "gone on too long" and should be halted?
6. Have you ever felt ashamed that you cried?
7. Have you ever felt that you should have cried when you didn't?
8. In referring to the Crying Scale on page 5, if you began to cry and you had a choice, what is the furthest step you would allow yourself to get to in public?

9. Same as #8; but, what step would you allow yourself to get to in private?

To some of these questions you may have answered, "no." But if you answered yes to any, then you have at least one rule, or more, for your crying behavior. For those questions where you answered yes, what does that tell you about yourself? For example, how do you feel about other people around you when you cry? Also, can you or should you work on changing your expectations of your crying, such as letting yourself cry or not cry?

"Too Much" Crying?

Is there such thing as too much crying? What about the person who cries five times a day for weeks or the person who cries for two hours straight? Isn't this too much? The only statement that we are going to make regarding "too much crying" is the following: A person's crying behavior has become unhealthy when it begins to interfere with their ability to complete the activities of daily living. That is, if a person's crying makes going to work, completing daily chores and interacting with others impossible, then he or she may need help. Otherwise, there is no such thing as "too much crying."

If the girlfriend of a fifteen year-old boy breaks off their relationship and the boy cries several times a day, who are we to say his crying is outside of an acceptable range? If a father of a twenty-year-old son who died last year cries much of the day on his son's twenty-first birthday, it is not our place to ask him to limit his tears.

Some of you may be just fine with your "frequent-crier" status while others may want to change. If you truly wish to cry less, then the advice opposite to the rare or no-criers applies to you: swallow when the tears start to come. Of course there appears to be a short-term cost for holding back tears. Remember when we talked about the basketball-size lump in your throat? However, the long-term effects of restricted crying have not been systematically investigated.

People Who Hold Back Tears

Do you want to cry, but find it's hard or you just can't? One way is to stand there and yell at yourself, "Come on. Cry! Cry!"

Rarely, however, does this work. If you wish to cry, but just feel "stuck" and can't seem to "get there" here are some suggestions:
- Give yourself permission to cry.
- Make sure that you are not trying to force an emotional response to please someone else.
- Find a safe environment. For most people, this is alone in their bedroom.
- For some, sitting in their car far from the view of others is an ideal place.
- In your room or car be sure to have music, a picture, a video, or other memory that has the ability to elicit sadness.
- Tell others in your household that you need privacy and not to come if they hear you or to call 911.
- As you experience sad thoughts, it is important to not engage in any hard swallowing or other distracting behaviors such as looking around, picking up something, doing Sudoku, or reading *The Wall Street Journal.*
- Be patient. Tears may not come right away.

However, if you are fine with your status, then it is the job of those around you to respect where you are in your responses to the joys and sorrows that come your way. Others may wish that you would "show your emotions" or "buck up." But you will do what you need to do when it comes to crying or not crying. Learn to accept your differences from other people and ask them to do the same.

CHAPTER 4: DEALING WITH CRYING

Clues to Tears

How might you detect the beginning of a cry? Here are some possible signs: (Note that some or all may be present)

- Glistening of the eyes. Look at the lower part of the eye for presence of fluid that was not present seconds before.
- Squinting of the eyes
- Increased blinking
- Reddening of the eyes
- Avoiding eye contact
- Reddening of the face
- Pursing of the lips
- Chin quivering
- Temporary suspension of breath
- Head moving down toward the chest; or in some cases moving upwards exposing the throat
- Sometimes one hand will cover part of the face

What to Do Once the Crying Begins

When the tears begin to flow, many people quickly appraise whether they are authentic or not [31]. Some people are reluctant to give criers the benefit of the doubt and they tend to see crying as more often consisting of "bad tears" (see page 15). They are more likely to use phrases that say, "turn off those tears." Others respond positively to tears and believe the crier deserves support. They are more likely to see crying in the "good tears" category and say things such as, "Go ahead and have a good cry."

If you've decided that the tears are authentic do all you can to avoid interfering with crying. A short poem may help you to remember this:

Let 'em cry
Until they're dry

This may be one of the most difficult things you do. An excellent piece of advice is to:

Allow the person to be in pain.

Some people say, "I can't stand to see another person crying, they will fall apart. What can I do?" If you truly want to be of service to other people, it is essential that you learn that you cannot take away another person's pain. Your job is to be there with them and to not interfere as they go through their difficult moments. This does not mean that you should stand there and do nothing. Of course if the person is in physical pain, find help. A headache usually calls for an aspirin. But with other pain, such as the pain of grief, it is vitally important to realize that you cannot "fix" it. Let's get specific:

If a person is crying in front of you and is talking through their tears about how much they miss their loved one, your job is to stand (or sit) and simply be a good listener without interfering with their words, tears, or anguish. To repeat: this apparent nonintervention may be some of the hardest work you will ever do. But, it must be done. Well-meaning helpers often try to offer words of "comfort" in an effort to stop or reduce the pain. Examples are:

Don't cry. (voted "worst sentence" by criers)
It'll be okay.
There, there, take it easy.

Okay, now wipe those tears.
You must pull yourself together.
You must be strong for your family.
I know just how you feel.
If you had more faith, you wouldn't be crying.
Everything will be all right.
Your loved one wouldn't want you to feel this way.
You wouldn't want your kids to see you cry.
At least....

If, in an attempt to comfort a person who has experienced a loss, you find yourself beginning your sentence with the words, "At least," you are likely headed for trouble. These two words imply that the grieving person should remember the positives that remain in their life; but that doesn't help. In fact, when you say "At least...." it often makes the person feel worse because you are minimizing their pain and dismissing their feelings. However, if the person crying says "At least....", then it's a different story. When you say it, you are not being helpful even if you think you are.

Sometimes people ask, "What happens if I start crying, too?" Our only rule here is: *Don't cry more than the other person.* Can you imagine? Here you are trying to be helpful to this person. He or she starts crying and you start boo-hooing. Then the person turns to you and tries to comfort you. So, stick by the rule: go ahead and cry *with*—but not *more*—than the crier.

What should you say when you see a person begin to cry? Here are some suggestions:
- Say nothing—Remember, your job is to do nothing to interfere with the crying process.
- Say, "It must be hard."
- Say, "It hurts, doesn't it?"

These last two sentences often lead to even more crying. It's okay to do this. The main thing to keep in mind is to not use words that will shorten or stop the crying process.

If you choose to touch the crying person, be sure it is gentle, tentative and appropriate and does *not* interfere with their tears. A light touch on the hand or shoulder may be okay, but a tight hug or a crushing and hearty pat on the back is more disruptive than supportive.

Self-Talk While Witnessing Crying

What should you say to yourself when you see a person begin to cry? Here are some suggestions: (make sure these self-talk phrases do not escape your lips)

Good.

This person is feeling their pain.

I need to just be here and let them cry.

I need to tolerate their pain because this is the best thing I can do for them at this moment.

It's okay. This person will stop at some point. Just wait patiently.

Where's my umbrella? (just kidding)

When You Are the One Crying

When the people you know see you cry, do they know exactly what to do? Consider doing the following:

Make a list of people who would likely see you cry. This may include the people you live with, family members, people at work and/or at church. Think about exactly what you would like them to do while you are crying. Then, contact each person and bring up the topic of crying and include what you would like the person to do and not do the next time you cry.

For those people in your life who tell you not to cry, here are some suggestions on what to say:

"I know you care, but it is okay for you to let me be in pain."

"I won't feel this lousy forever."

"If you stop me from crying, it won't make me feel any better."

"Please understand that telling me not to cry only makes me feel worse; and telling me that it's okay to cry actually makes me feel better."

"There are a lot more tears where these came from. So, get ready."

Sign Language in the Midst of Tears

What if you are crying and a well-meaning friend runs up and hugs you, effectively stopping your tears? Or what if you are crying and you want a hug? What to do? We have created special hand signals for just such a situation. The big problem is that in the middle of our crying episode, we may not remember the signs. Or if we do, we won't have the wherewithal to even begin to display the proper sign. Despite these problems, we're going forth with our version of crying signs. Given that they only take a second to display, these signs might actually work for one person in a hundred. With that said, here are the signs:

- Arm extended, palm facing toward the other person says, "Stay away."
- Hand in front of face, palm facing towards face with *fore*finger wagging says, "Come comfort me."
- Forefingers inserted into both ears say, "Shut up. Read *The Crying Handbook*."

Your job is to convey the meaning of these special hand signals ahead of time to everyone you know. Even better, create one of those forward/forward/forward emails and send it around the world. Think of all the good luck you will have at the same time you will be getting your crying needs met.

Breathing After Crying

A few minutes after crying, a breathing exercise can sometimes be helpful. Here are three excellent examples. To avoid light-headedness, never do two in succession.

1. *Deep Breath*. Take a deep breath, hold it—then take in a little more and then a little more. Exhale and breathe normally.
2. *Focused Breathing*. Close your eyes and "see" your breath move in and out of your nostrils or your mouth. As you inhale, say your name in your mind. As you exhale, say "Relax." Do this 5-10 times. Then breathe normally.
3. *Ratio Breathing*. Inhale for a count of "4." Hold your breath for a count of "16." Exhale for a count of "8." Breath normally.

Don't try this one: Breathe in.

Be Prepared for Tears

Always carry sufficient tissues. Have you ever noticed that in the United States, we ask to "borrow a tissue"? Do we really want to *borrow* a tissue or are we just being polite? If you do not wish to carry 100 of those little tissue packs, then be more practical and use toilet tissue. You could grab some off the roll each morning and stuff it into your pocket. (No one will say anything to you.

Surely you have seen people come out of the restroom with a piece of toilet tissue stuck on their shoe and *no one* says anything to them....). Or you could simply carry a roll of tissue around with you. If people ask you what you are doing with the toilet tissue, simply reply "I am prepared" and no one will ask any more questions!

- Do not use articles of clothing to sop up the tears. See above
- Do not use table cloths, placemats or chair doilies (napkins, however, are okay) Tears may stain and you do not want permanent reminders of your sob fest.
- If you are going to cry, then no sniveling. When you attempt to lessen the number or amount of tears, you end up making some very strange and unattractive sounds (see *The Hiccupper,* page 29) and your nose drips...not a good picture. Cry or don't, but don't do anything half way.
- Try not to fall into someone else while crying. Sometimes we are so overwhelmed with our tears that we may tend to fall forward into someone's chest, which, depending upon that person's height, could be embarrassing. If you are a female, you might also run the risk of sharing your make-up with that person's shirt or jacket...not a good idea. (If you are in the role of a crier support person, you may wish to consider wearing make-up colored clothing or a large apron)
- Remember that you owe *no one* an explanation for your tears. If you wish to share with someone the reasons for your tears, go ahead. But you do not have to explain tears to anyone.
- Do not apologize for crying (unless you have disrupted the second act of a great play, ruined a wedding ceremony or fallen face forward into the salad). You never have to apologize for what you feel. You may, however, have to apologize for what you *do* with what you feel. Unless you

acted in a totally unacceptable manner, let the tears speak for themselves. If you must explain, a simple "I'm just having a (choose one or more) sad/bad/hard/difficult moment. Thanks for asking."

- If you believe your crying is disruptive or unsettling to others, you may wish to find a private place to cry. Some churches and theaters have Cry Rooms (usually utilized by young mothers with crying babies, but who cares...tears are tears, no matter who is shedding them). Excusing yourself from a gathering is certainly acceptable, especially if you can do so gracefully. Running, screaming from the building would not fall into the graceful category.

- Some find excusing themselves to "use the restroom" works well. Few people question that.

CHAPTER 5: STORIES OF CRYING

Thirty years ago my husband and I experienced the death of our second child, a son, at the age of thirteen months. Austin died of a malignant brain tumor and left a four-year-old "Big Sister" and the two of us to wander through the uncharted territory of grief. There were few resources to help us and little understanding about grief. We became lost and our world began to come apart.

After months of trying to ease each other's pain, my husband and I began to turn away from each other and we became strangers. We decided to end the pain and get divorced. We were so hurt that we could not even agree on how to divide up the world we had built together. We fought over everything, including the dishes, the silverware and the pictures. We had collected Navajo rugs and had been given an especially nice antique one as a wedding present. It became the final decision to be made before the split was finalized.

We simply could not decide how to divide the rug and the arguments grew loud and vicious. We poured all our hurt into that one rug. Finally, in a moment of pure insanity, I grabbed a pair of scissors and started to cut the rug in half. This was an antique, a truly beautiful piece of art and I had already cut two threads before the absurdity of it cut through my "fog." I stopped and began to laugh at how silly we both were being: to destroy a piece of antiquity simply because two grown-ups could not decide who should "keep it!"

I sat on the bare living room floor and laughed and laughed. Gradually my husband joined me in the laughter. We laughed as we had not laughed in months. Tears streamed down our faces as our laughter opened the floodgates of emotion and we were really crying. Neither of us wanted a divorce. We just didn't recognize each other any more. We were strangers to each other. We were strangers to ourselves. Grief had left us empty and hollow and alone in our pain and sorrow.

And so, in those tearful hours after I nearly destroyed a beautiful piece of history, we began to talk. Out poured the sorrow, the bitterness, the despair, the grief. We decided to give ourselves 365 days to see if we could repair the hurts and the tears in our family fabric. If we could not, then we would divorce because two adults could not make it, not because one little boy had died.

It was one of the best laughs we have ever had together and the best tears we shed. One door opened—the door to the buried hurts and sorrow—and once the tears began, we learned not to judge each other by the number of tears that flowed down our cheeks.

I am a Weeper and a Wailer and my husband is a Non-crier. You can imagine the misinterpretations we each made about the other. He thought I was too emotional and unstable and I thought he didn't love our son and didn't care that he was dead. How wrong we both were! And we almost let our misunderstandings about the way people cry (or don't cry) destroy the family we were.

Now, 36 years later, we honor and cherish our differences rather than use them as weapons.
Darcie

More stories continued..........

47

We are grateful to these people who were willing to share their own tear story. They illustrate so beautifully many of the ideas we have explored in this book. The stories are as unique as the individuals who have shared them and they remind us that there are many paths that lead to tears.

There wasn't much I could do...

I was in Valley Medical Center Critical Care Unit with my grandmother after her stroke. My parents, brother, my brother's best friend, cousins, and my uncle and aunt were with me. I delayed my tears during the time when the doctors were taking my grandmother off of life support and putting her to sleep forever. But as soon as I hugged and kissed my grandmother for the last time, I couldn't resist crying. Grief triggered my tears, and it was impossible to stop. My tears were rolling down my cheeks. All I know is I cried a lot.

I was in my deepest level of grief. I was stressed out as well. I felt as if God had played an unfair game with me. My grandmother should've lived a few more years. I stood there with my close family members around me. They were all crying as well. I think I only cry when there is no other solution to my problem. Here it was my grandmother who was going away from me and there wasn't much I could do, but cry.

Rupan

It's usually frustration...

The last time I threw a fit, screaming and wailing and gnashing of teeth I was about five. Since then, I only cry when I'm frustrated or grievously injured. Since I'm not terribly accident prone, it's usually frustration that leads me to cry. When I argue about any topic with a certain person in my life—who was in a movie, who should win a political race, what I should do with my life—he doesn't fight fair. And when he ends a fight or argument trying to establish his authority instead of with facts or logic, especially when I know I'm right, and more importantly, that he is wrong, I get upset. But since I can't argue anymore, all the tension I've built up in the last few minutes just has to come out somehow. I try to stop it, because I hate crying, I get nauseous and I get a headache. My throat gets so tight I can't breath and my eyes sting and my nose starts to run—I'm not a pretty crier. I usually try to leave the scene before the tears start falling. A few tears fall and my breath hitches and I blow my nose and feel ridiculous for taking it so personally and for being so hell-bent on winning an argument that I lose my cool. And then we start it all again in a few weeks or months.

Lacinda

After today, no longer would my tears be publicly acceptable. The flag was folded and presented. The 21-gun salute shattered the stillness and TAPS faded away. "My silent tears gave way to a hesitant voice and then suddenly, we were all singing God Bless America as loud as we could… grief echoing over the graves, a public love affair for a private hurt." It was now finished. A final good-bye and now our grief was to be over. We left the cemetery to join others for a gathering meant to turn the sadness of the day into a celebration of life. But no amount of casserole or chocolate could keep my attention from wandering back to that place where both my husband and father lay together…. Rest in Peace.

For three days our pain and sorrow was accepted, even encouraged. But now, with the last hug given, the last dish washed, I knew our grief would no longer be acceptable. The death of our loved one had gone, in the space of three days, from private to public and back again. After today, no longer would my tears be publicly acceptable. Grief was to go silent as we were expected to "get on with our lives".

Why must grief go into hiding? Why, after three or four days—a week at most, is grief expected to move from public display to private anguish?

Joyce

...and only then not until I was positive that I was alone.
When I was seven years old, my father was killed by a drunk driver. He was only thirty-one. I learned about his death the morning after it happened. I remember my mother calling me downstairs; and, as I entered the living room, I was surprised to see my favorite uncle standing there next to her. My surprise quickly turned to confusion as I noticed that both my mother and uncle were crying. I asked what was wrong and that was when they told me that my father was dead.

I don't think many seven year olds understand the concept of death—I know I didn't. I did not understand that this terrible news meant that I would never see my father alive again, which may be why I did not cry as my heartbroken mother and uncle broke the news. I recall my mother telling me that it was all right to cry but still I did not. In fact, I didn't cry until after the funeral, and only then not until I was positive that I was alone. I have always wondered why that is.

I do know that it was not until after I viewed my father's lifeless but peaceful body lying in the casket that I truly understood the reality of the situation as well as what it meant to be dead. Still, why did I wait to cry until I was alone? I was never brought up to believe boys were not supposed to cry. To this day, I can count on one hand the number of times I have cried about my father's death in the presence of another person. It is not that I did not love my father, he was my hero. Since my father's passing I have suffered other losses of loved ones, each with little or no outward show of emotion.

With no personal history of abuse or neglect, and a relatively normal childhood, I have no explanation for my bottling up my emotions. I have no doubt that my father's death has influenced how I react emotionally to personal loss, but what I can not figure out is my reaction to what has been, up to this point in my life, the greatest loss I have ever experienced.
Robert

I tried to tell him she had passed, but I just broke down...
The summer I had turned 13, my Great Aunt Jeanie entered a nursing home. I had gone to visit her a few times and one of those times she looked more worn than usual. We stayed and talked for a while and just before I left, she grabbed my hand as I sat next to her. She looked me right in the eyes and said "You'll come visit me one more time before I die won't you, Jill?" I looked at her and instantly replied, "Yes." I didn't expect her to be going anywhere anytime soon. "Promise?" She asked with a smile on her face. And with a smile back I replied, "I promise."

That next weekend my mom asked me if I wanted to go and visit Aunt Jeanie, I declined the opportunity. I figured I'd just go the weekend after. Around the middle of the week after my mom had gone to see her, she called me and was crying hysterically. I couldn't understand her. Finally she got it out, Aunt Jeanie had passed away. I nearly dropped the phone. I couldn't say anything to my mom. She was upset that I wasn't talking and that I wasn't crying. She was yelling at me, but I couldn't feel anything. I was numb. I got off the phone with my mom and sat there for a minute. I wasn't able to believe it was happening. But still, I couldn't cry. I saw my friend Nick next door outside mowing the lawn. He knew what was going on with Aunt Jeanie. He was my best friend. I walked outside and started walking towards him. He saw me and must have seen the look on my face. Instantly he turned the mower off and started walking towards me.

As I got closer to him Aunt Jeanie's voice inquisitively asking "Promise?" echoed in my mind. I tried to tell him she had passed but I just broke down and sobbed my eyes out. He just stood there, held me, and stroked my hair. He was able to calm me down and ask me if I wanted to talk to his mother, but I didn't. To this day it hurts me to think I never got to see her that one last time. But I know that she knows it wasn't intentional. Someday I will see her again and that's not a promise, that's a guarantee.
Jill

I learned that if I suppress things for too long...
I was 16, and in my room alone at two or three in the morning and listening to music. I began thinking about the past and living in Miami and all the physical and emotional pain I had been through, when I started to cry. I tried not to because crying has never been a good thing to do because my family always says how soft you are and if you were stable you wouldn't be crying. So I attempted to keep myself from crying as long as possible, but I kept having these negative visions play over and over and over in my head. I couldn't help it. I just started wailing like a baby. I was crying so much I couldn't catch my breath.

After about 30 minutes, I started screaming about how unfair this was and why did this have to be me? Why would this happen to anyone? At first I tried to keep from crying, I tried to stop myself, but then I just let go. I figured since every one was sleeping no one would be upset about it. I felt extremely embarrassed that I was crying, and even more so that I was crying like a baby, even including yelling for "mommy." When it was all over I felt a little better because it had been so very long since I last cried. I felt relief, but I still felt horrible, mostly because it had taken me months to react to what had been done to me for so long. I learned that if I suppress things for too long that I would eventually burst. I must let my feelings through when it comes to that and not hold them in.
Jessie

But hearing myself say it aloud was exponentially worse...
The event in question happened when I was 17. My girlfriend at the time and I had sustained a long distance relationship for roughly 11 months but it had been getting more and more difficult. I had just walked into the movies with my dad and step-mom when my phone rang. It was my girlfriend and she seemed somewhat depressed. I asked her what was wrong, and her exact response was, "I'm sad because we're breaking up..." Needless to say I was surprised. So naturally I questioned it as calmly as I could. After asking a few futile questions I just said I'd talk to her later because there had been this horrible pain in my stomach/chest. It felt a lot like an ulcer, and it was weighing me down more than the shock of being told I'd been dumped by someone I loved enough to spend every cent I had flying down every other month.

I felt numb for about 5 minutes, leaning against the lobby wall, except the painful tinge in my torso. I tried calling a couple of friends but nobody was answering, so I set my phone to vibrate and tried to watch the movie. When a friend returned my call about 20 minutes into the movie, I walked out to the lobby and answered the phone. As I attempted to say "Hi," my eyes immediately began to well up, my throat choked, I started shaking slightly, and even began sobbing. Every time I tried to speak to my friend I would choke up again. It took a good five minutes, but I was finally able to explain to her what had happened. However, every time my girlfriend's name came up, I would choke up worse than before. I knew that what had happened was real, but hearing myself say it aloud was exponentially worse than just knowing. Despite my best efforts, I couldn't keep all my tears back. After about 10 minutes of that, I was so drained I wanted to lie down on the lobby floor and just wanted to give up, even though there was nothing to give up on. My friend was sympathetic. She didn't rush me. She didn't try to push anything on me. She just let me know she cared and felt for me. Finally when I stopped, I didn't feel bad, but I didn't feel better. I had gone from numb, to pain, to being completely drained and I didn't feel that I had anything left in me.

Richard

After I finished I felt foolish...

The time in my life when I cried the most was surprising. I have twelve siblings, eleven living, one dead. My missing sibling is my littlest brother Jacob, who would be about nine years old now. When he died three days after his birth I was about nine years old, and I wore a pink dress to his funeral. It was my first experience with death, and the first funeral I'd been to, so I didn't quite understand what it meant for him to be dead. He didn't feel real to me then; and all that I felt was disappointment that I wouldn't get to play with him. In more recent years I've thought about him, cried a little (never more than a few tears quickly wiped), and thought that I'd accepted pretty well that he was real, and he was gone, and I would be with him when I died.

When I was sixteen, I was at a weeklong girls' camp. During the torch ceremony two girls that I casually knew had just discovered that their sister's baby daughter had died a few hours after being born. I couldn't think of anything to say to comfort them, and I didn't know them well enough to give hugs. I then began to think about my four darling nieces and my brother Jacob, and how much pain those two girls must be in, and I started crying. I can hardly describe how I felt. The closest feeling would be a combination of frustration and longing. I was standing in line with a torch, and I tried really hard to stop crying or at least seem like I wasn't, but a friend behind me noticed and asked if I was okay, which made me cry harder. I told her about my little brother and the two girls' niece, and she hugged me and told me about an experience of hers; and I was able to stop crying. After I was finished I felt foolish, because I was crying about two girls I hardly knew, and for a brother who had been gone for many years. But when I think about that day and how I felt, and those girls, my eyes still start to water and I have to fight to not cry. I don't even understand why that affects me so much, because I've heard of much worse things and not felt even close to crying.
Amy

...sometimes it felt like I would cry forever.
I had a major falling out with my boyfriend and cried for days straight to the point where I couldn't go to school or work. When I finally was brave enough to get out of the house there were times in school or at work when it was so hard to hold back my tears. Doing everyday things would make me break into tears. But I held back my tears because even though I wasn't over the pain, I

was obligated to go through my everyday life. I would drive in my car and it was like a safety zone where I could cry and scream and yell and cry some more. Some times I would take a drive to an empty parking lot just to cry. It was such a relief. It felt so good to cry because after I did, it made me feel empty inside which was better than feeling all that pain and hurt welled up inside. I cried and it was a temporary relief.

There were times when my family would try and comfort me and I would cry into my mother's arms. I would cry and I felt like I didn't care who saw but after a while I would start to hold back my tears. To be alone and cry allowed me to cry for as long as I wanted and as loud as I wanted. It was such a relief and it is as human as you can get! People need to cry some more and stop judging others who cry. I don't really know when or how I stopped crying but sometimes it felt like I would cry forever. I guess I learned to adjust to it. I started talking to my boyfriend again which helped because even though we weren't together it was good to have someone know what I was going through and how low I was feeling. I didn't think I couldn't talk to anyone else because I felt like they would judge me, especially if I started crying.

There are very few people who I would feel comfortable crying my eyes out to and those are people who will comfort me but at the same time just let me cry and not say a word about it. I don't remember the last time I cried like this. It was when I was a child and scraped knees were something to cry about. But this uncontrollable crying helped me to remember what a relief it is to let out all those balled up feelings. And crying may not make the pain go away but at least it lets it out from inside of you.
Candi

CHAPTER 6: AN IDEAL CRYING SOCIETY

Of course "ideal" depends upon each society. But we'll try to convey a little of what we personally hope for. In our ideal society we would see crying as a normal human expression. Yet, for those who don't cry or cry little, we would show the utmost tolerance and acceptance. When a person in our midst begins to cry, we would do nothing to interfere with its full expression and everything to support it. As a society we would not be fearful allowing a person unlimited crying except in the rare cases where it interfered with their daily activities. We would understand that no one cries forever. People live in a healthy society when its citizens are not afraid to display their full expression of pain, sorrow and joy.

> *Tears on the outside*
> *Fall to the ground*
> *And are slowly swept away.*
> *Tears on the inside*
> *Fall on the soul*
> *And stay and stay and stay.*
>
> *Donald Wayne Rash*

In our ideal society, we would not have to "borrow" tissues, hide our tears or apologize if we don't cry. Crying would be as natural as children laughing and people singing. In our ideal society we would begin to understand that, when someone loses "it" perhaps they are really finding "it" instead. It would be a real and honest and compassionate world. We hope we all find it soon.

POSTSCRIPT

You have just finished a book about crying. Good for you. In it, we have explored the definitions of crying, myths, a brief history and the cultural influences of crying. Research on crying as a social phenomenon, crying on the Big Screen and differences in crying were examined. We looked at types of criers, how to determine how much or how little crying is "socially acceptable" and triggers for crying. We discussed personal rules for crying and how to deal with tears, both our own and those of others. We shared some "tear stories" and made suggestions for an ideal crying society.

More than a compilation of facts and research, we hope this book has become a guide for something much more than information. We hope that you feel it has been about you. Consider using the Personal Crying Survey on the next page to help deepen understanding of your own tears and those of others. As Kottler asks in his book, *The Language of Tears*, what are you going to do with what you have learned?

Now that you have read *The Crying Handbook*, will you just close it and put it back on the shelf or can it become something more? Will this book help you to become more aware of how you respond to your own tears? Will it help you grow more comfortable with the way others cry or do not cry? Can it help you make a difference in the way you regard your own crying style?

We appreciate your willingness to travel with us on this journey of tears. Don't forget to bring the tissues, a sense of humor, your sense of compassion and caring for yourself and others. And don't forget a good pair of walking shoes. Journey well.

APPENDIX: PERSONAL CRYING SURVEY

If your tears could talk, what would they say to you? Do you have the courage to listen? These questions might help you better understand your own personal crying style. It might help to start a conversation with yourself (and perhaps others) about what you believe and feel about crying.

1. What are my current triggers that bring tears? (refer to pages 32 and 33).
2. What is the best place for me to cry?
3. What is the worst place?
4. With whom should I talk regarding my crying (or theirs)?
5. What are my concerns about crying?
6. The hardest person for me to see crying is_____.
7. The person who would find it hardest to see me crying is _____.
8. If I am not a crier, how should I tell people that it's certainly okay *not* to cry?

REFERENCES

[1] Vingerhoets, A.J.J.M., Boelhouwer, A.J.W., Van Tilburg, M.A.L., & Van Heck, G.L., (2001). The situational and emotional context of adult crying. In *Adult Crying: A Biopsychosocial Approach*, Ad. J.J.M. Vingerhoets & Randolph R. Cornelius (Eds.), Brunner-Routledge Publishers (an imprint of the Taylor & Francis Group, Philadelphia).

[2] Lofgren, L.B. (1966). On weeping. *International Journal of Psychoanalysis, 47*, 375-383.

[3] Stearns, P.N. & Knapp, M. (1996). Historical perspectives on grief. In R. Harre & W.G. Parrot (Eds.) *The Emotions: Social, Cultural, and Biological Dimensions*. London, UK: Sage.

[4] Krugman,, R.D. (1983-85). Fatal child abuse: Analysis of 24 cases. *Pediatrician, 12*, 68-72.

[5] Schmitt, B.D. (1985). Colic: Excessive crying in newborns. *Clinics in Perinatology, 12*, 441-451.

[6] Van Haeringen, N.J. (1981). Clinical biochemistry of tears. *Survey of Ophthalmology, 26*, 84-96.

[7] Lutz, T. (1999). *Crying: The Natural & Cultural History of Tears.* New York: W.W. Norton.

[8] Frey, W.H., Desota Johnson, D., Hoffman, C., & McCall, J.T. (1981). Effect of stimulus on the chemical composition of human tears. *American Journal of Ophthalmology, 92*, 559-567.

[9] Frey, W.H., Nilson, J.D., Frich, M.L., & Elde, R.P. (1986). Prolactin immunoreactivity in human tears and lacrimal gland: Possible implications for tear production. In: F.J. Holly (Ed.), *The Preocular Tear Film in Health, Disease, and Contact Lens Wear,* (798-807). Lubbock, TX: Dry Eye Institute.

[10] Lensvelt, G. & Vingerhoets, A.J.J.M. (1998). Unpublished data.

[11] Vingerhoets, A.J.J.M., Van Tilburg, M.A.L., Boelhouwer, A.J.W. & Van Heck, G.L. (2001). Personality and Crying. In *Adult Crying: A Biopsychosocial Approach*, Ad. J.J.M. Vingerhoets & Randolph R.Cornelius (Eds.), Brunner-Routledge Publishers.

[12] Frey (1985) Crying: *The Mystery of Tears*. Minneapolis, MN: Winston Press.

[13] Vingerhoets, A.J.J.M., Van Geleuken, A.J.M.L., Van Tilburg, M.A.L., & Van Heck, G.L. (1997). The psychological context of crying episodes: Toward a model of adult crying. In: A.J.J.M. Vingerhoets, F.J. Van Bussel, & A.J.W. Boelhouwer (Eds.), *The (Non)expression of Emotions in Health and Disease* (pp. 323-336). Tilburg, The Netherlands: Tilburg University Press.

[14] Becht, M. & Vingerhoets, A.J.J.M. (1997). *Why we cry and how it affects mood*. Paper presented at the Annual Meeting of the American Psychosomatic Society, Sante Fe, NM (Abstracted in *Psychosomatic Medicine*, *59*, 92)

[15] Van Tilburg, M.A.L. & Vingerhoets, A.J.J.M. (2000).Menstrual cycle, mood, and crying. *Psychosomatic Medicine*, *62*, 146.

[16] Delp, M.J. & Sackeim, H.A. (1987). Effects of mood on lacrimal flow: Sex differences and asymmetry. *Psychophysiogy*, *24*, 550-556.

[17] Labott, S.M. & Martin, R.B. (1988). Weeping, evidence for a cognitive theory: *Motivation and Emotion*, *12*, 205-216.

[18] Kottler, J.A. (1996). *The Language of Tears*. San Francisco: Jossey-Bass.

[19] Doherty, R.W., Oroimoto, L., Singelis, T.M., Hatfield, E., & Hebb, J.(1995). Emotional contagion: Gender and occupational differences. *Psychology of Women Quarterly*, *19*, 355-371.

[20] Hatfield, E., Cacioppo, J.T., & Rapson, R.L. (1994). *Emotional Contagion*. NY: Cambridge University Press.

[21] Vingerhoets, A.J.J.M., Van Tilburg, M.A., Boelhouwer, A.J.W., & Van Heck, G.L.(2001). Personality and Crying. In *Adult Crying: A Biopsychosocial Approach*. Asd. J.J.M. Vingerhoets & Randolph R. Conrelius (Eds.) Brunner-Routledge Publishers (an imprint of the Taylor & Francis Group).

[22] Wellenkamp, J.C. (1988). Notions of grief and catharsis among the Toraja. *American Ethnologist*, *15*, 486-500.

[23] Vingerhoets, A.J.J.M. & Becht, M.C. (1996, August). The ISAC study: Some preliminary findings. International Conference on the (Non) Expression of Emotions. In Health and Disease. Tilburg University, The Netherlands.(Abstract in *Psychosomatic Medicine*, *59*, 85-86).

[24] Guyda, H.J. & Friesen, H.G. (1973). Serum prolactin levels in humans from birth to adult life. *Pediatric Research*, *7*, 534-540.

[25] Jacobs, L.S., Mariz, I.K., & Daughaday, W.H. (1972). A mixed heterologous radioimmunoassay for human prolactin. *Journal of Clinical Endocrinology*, *34*, 484-490.

[26] Hastrup, J.L., Kraemer, D.T., Bornstein, R.F., & Trezza, G..R. (2001). Crying frequency across the lifespan. In *Adult Crying: A Biopsychosocial Approach*, Ad. J.J.M. Vingerhoets & Randolph R. Cornelius (Eds.), Brunner-Routledge Publishers (an imprint of the Taylor & Francis Group).

[27] Frey, W.H., Hoffman-Ahern, C., Johnson, R.A., Lykken, D.T. & Tuason, V.B. (1983). Crying behavior in the human adult. *Integrative Psychiatry*, *1*, 94-98.

[28] Williams, D.G. & Morris, G.H. (1996). Crying, weeping or tearfulness in British and Israeli adults. *British Journal of Psychology*, *87*, 479-505.

[29] Chupak, Cindy (1994). Can you stand to see a grown man cry? *Glamour Magazine*, 128.

[30] Koestler, Arthur (1964). *The Art of Creation*. NY: Penguin.

[31] Tomkins, S. (1962-92). *Affect, Imagery, Consciousness* (4 volume set). NY: Springer.

ACKNOWLEDGMENTS

Thanks to the many criers and noncriers alike who gave us input on drafts of this book:

Jim Baugher	Robert Kralis
Karen Brown	Diane Knox
Wendy Buck	Joe Kristofzski
Jill Calahan	Marci Kristofzski
Michael Campbell	Maureen Kristofzski
Amy Collier	Mike McDowell
Randolph R. Cornelius, Ph.D.	Nancy Parker McGlynn
Elaine Eggebraaten	Lacinda Mennenga
Marilyn Evans	Denise Montoya
Natalie Fisher	Mushroom Montoya
Alicia S. Franklin	Candi Rosario
Anne Hallman	Robert A. (Tony) Sims
Rupan Heyar	Richard Squires
Di Jones	Carol Sunada
Bob Keene	Deborah D. Switzer
Jeff Keller	Dorothy J. Williams-Dotson
Lori Keller	Jessica Word

Special thanks to our editor, Andrea Gambill.

Thanks also to Bob's wife, Kris, for her computer, production, and design expertise in preparing this book for printing.

ABOUT THE AUTHORS

Bob Baugher

Bob Baugher, Ph.D. is a psychologist and certified death educator who teaches at Highline Community College in Des Moines, Washington. He is a 20-year member of the advisory committee of the South King County Chapter of The Compassionate Friends. In 2001 Bob was presented with The Compassionate Friends Professional Award. Bob has given more than 400 workshops, was a clinician with the University of Washington Parent Bereavement Project, and has co-facilitated children's grief support groups. He is a trainer for the Washington State Youth Suicide Prevention Program and has trained more than 1,000 people in suicide intervention. Bob has written several articles on grief, including a research piece entitled, *How Long (According to the Media) Should Grief Last?* He is co-author of six other books: *A Guide for the Bereaved Survivor*, *A Guide to Understanding Guilt during Bereavement*, *Understanding Anger during Bereavement*, *Death Turns Allie's Family Upside Down* (a child's book on death), *Coping with Traumatic Death: Homicide*, and *After Suicide Loss: Coping with Your Grief.*

Darcie D. Sims

Darcie D. Sims, Ph.D., CHT, CT, GMS is a bereaved parent and child, a grief management specialist, a nationally certified thanatologist, a certified pastoral bereavement specialist and a licensed psychotherapist and hypnotherapist. She is the author of *Why Are the Casseroles Always Tuna?*, *Footsteps Through the Valley*, *Touchstones* and *If I Could Just See Hope.* She co-authored *A Place For Me: A Healing Journey for Grieving Kids*, *Footsteps Through Grief*, *The Other Side of Grief* and *Finding Your Way Through Grief* with her daughter, Alicia Sims Franklin. She wrote and produced the videos *Handling the Holidays* and *What Color is Dead: Death From A Child's View* and is featured in the award-winning video series "*Good Grief*" and in several other videos. She was Coping Editor for *Bereavement* magazine for 15 years and is now an editor for *Grief Digest.* Darcie received The Compassionate Friends Professional Award in 1999, is president and co-founder of GRIEF, Inc. a grief consulting business and the Director of the American Grief Academy in Seattle, Washington.

The following materials written by Dr. Darcie D. Sims are available at
www.Griefstore.com. Or by calling (253) 929-0649.

Why Are The Casseroles Always Tuna?
$9.95

If I Could Just See Hope
$14.00

Footsteps Through Grief with Alicia S. Franklin
$9.00

The Other Side of Grief with Alicia S. Franklin
$9.00

Finding Your Way Through Grief CD with Alicia S. Franklin
$12.00

A Place For Me: A Healing Journey For Kids Ages 8-80
(meditation tape)
$10.00

Touchstones
(packet of inspirational sayings on wallet size cards)
$5.00

Handling the Holidays (DVD)
$30.00

What Color Is Dead? Death From A Child's View (video)
$50.00

She can be contacted at Darcie@Griefinc.com or
by calling (253) 929-0649

Visit her website at www.GriefInc.com

DISCOUNTS FOR ORDERING MULTIPLE COPIES
OF THE CRYING HANDBOOK

2-10 copies	5% Discount
11-24 copies	10% Discount
25-49 copies	20% Discount
50-99 copies	30% Discount
100 or more	35% Discount

Price: $10.00 (U.S. funds) per copy
Add $2.00 postage for a single copy
Free postage for U.S. orders of 2 or more copies
Shipping: Canadian and out of U.S. orders will be billed
according to postal rates.

WASHINGTON STATE RESIDENTS ADD 9% SALES TAX
Please allow 2-4 weeks for delivery

Send Check or Money Order to:
Bob Baugher, Ph.D.
7108 127ᵗʰ Place SE
Newcastle, WA 98056-1325
or
email your order and you will be billed
b_kbaugher@yahoo.com

OTHER BOOKS BY DR. BOB BAUGHER:

- *A Guide for the Bereaved Survivor* with Marc Calija
- *A Guide to Understanding Guilt during Bereavement*
- *Understanding Anger during Bereavement* with Carol and Gary Hankins
- *Death Turns Allie's Family Upside Down* with Linda Wong-Garl and Kristina J. Baugher
- *Coping with Traumatic Death: Homicide* with Lew Cox
- *After Suicide: Coping with Your Grief* with Jack Jordan

Pricing and taxes subject to change without notice